# New Perspectives: Domestic interiors

Work Conception: Arian Mostaedi
Editor: Carles Broto
Editorial Coordinator: Cristina Soler
Architecture adviser: Eduard Malgosa
Graphic Design: Oriol Vallès Garcia
Texts: Contributed by the architects


© Links International
Junqueres 10. 1-5.
08003 Barcelona. Spain
tel: +34 93 301 21 99
fax: + 34 93 301 00 21
info@linksbooks.net
www.linksbooks.net

Edition 2007



No part of this publication may be reproduced, stored in retrieval system or transmitted in any form or means, electronic, mechanical, photocopying, recording or otherwise, without the prior permission of th owner of the Copyright.

# New Perspectives: Domestic interiors

# Index

8 **Thomas Hanrahan & Victoria Meyers.** *Loft Holley*

22 **Christa Prantl & Alexander Runser.** *Lanzendorfer Mühle*

30 **Sergio Calatroni.** *Casa Galleria Uchida*

38 **Circus Architects.** *Vaight Apartment*

50 **Rüdiger Lainer.** *Peinthouse Seilergasse*

58 **Engelen Moore.** *House in Redfern*

68 **Landau & Kindelbacher.** *Housing Conversion*

76 **Cesare Leonardi.** *Mescoli-Goich House*

88 **Adolf H. Kelz & Hubert Soran.** *Mittermayer House*

96 **Michael Photiadis.** *House in Ekali*

106 **Claudio Silvestrin.** *Thames Apartment*

114 **Marc van Schuylenbergh.** *Conversion of Van Schuylenbergh House*

122 **Arthur Collin architect.** *Loft Apartment in Clerkenwell*

130 **Valerio Dewalt Train.** *Gardner Residence*

142 **Rataplan.** *Studio flat*
156 **Simon Conder & Associates.**
*Flat Conversion in Primrose Hill*
164 **Claeson, Koivisto & Rune.** *Apartment in Stockholm*
172 **Torsten Neeland.** *House of Dr. Shank*
182 **Fritz & Elizabeth Barth.** *Artists' studio*
194 **Giovanni Scheibler.** *Loft Conversion in Zurich*
200 **Paul Robbrecht & Hilde Daem.** *The Mys House*
210 **Ian Hay.** *Hay Apartment*
218 **Hermann & Valentiny.** *Anna House*
230 **Waro Kishi & K. Associates .** *House in Shimogamo*
238 **Eduard Broto.** *Studio in Eixample*
246 **Massimo e Gabriella Carmassi.** *Two Apartments in Pisa*

# *Introduction*

Interior design is one of the areas of architecture that has evolved most over the last few decades. New trends and lines of development can clearly be seen in the materials used, construction methods and styles.

In response to demanding clients with a wide range of requirements, architects working in interior design have had to explore new fields, opening up new paths that respond to the tastes and needs of new generations. The basic challenge is usually to interpret and add creative value to the needs of the client, who will often be excessively preoccupied with the purely commercial aspects or lured by fleeting fashions. This is why in good interior design there is always evidence of the effort to achieve the perfect synthesis between function and aesthetics, the essential and the non-essential.

This book contains solutions of the most diverse types, but it may be possible to identify a few tendencies that could be considered common to the new generations of interior design: a tendency to leave spaces clear of decorative objects that conceal the architectural lines, the almost total elimination of the elements commonly used to distinguish load-bearing structures, a clear tendency towards open spaces with few spatial divisions, and the recurring use of light and color as an integral part of the architectural solution.

In short, this book presents a selection of the most interesting examples of interior design created in the nineties, illustrating a return to more humanized concepts based on the profound relationship between man and the space he inhabits.

# Thomas Hanrahan & Victoria Meyers

## Holley Loft
*New York, USA*

*Photographs: Peter Aaron / Esto*

This project is an adaptation of an existing 4000 ft2 industrial loft space into a residence. The space is on the second floor of a loft building in lower Manhattan. In the final design, no solid walls were left. A single full-height wall of glass and steel marked the major division of master bedroom and bathroom from the rest of the apartment. From any position, the intention is to experience the full dimension of the entire loft space, with all the elements of the program distributed freely in the form of low cabinetry and movable panels. This disposition yields a complex space of constantly changing perspectives and points of view. Light from the short ends of the apartment penetrates deep into the residence, while the movable panels allow for the creation of smaller, more intimate spaces to accommodate overnight guests.

The major division within the space is made by a 48ft long raw steel and glass wall. This marks the division between the master bedroom/master bath area and the rest of the apartment with sandblasted areas for privacy. The area covered by the curtain is clear glass. The movement of the curtain allows the inhabitant of the space to control its openness.

Opposite the steel and glass wall is a 30ft long maple cabinet, which contains an objectified fragment of the steel and glass wall plane. Here, in order to mark its displacement, the wall curves. This cabinet also marks a boundary between the living spaces and a kitchen/guest bath. Translucent materials hang through a wood cabinet at specific locations to partially reveal the space beyond.

Full-height painted wood panels can either close down the rear of the apartment or remain in a fully open position. When they are open the panels float in the space: closed they demarcate one room; closed further, two rooms. The disposition of these spaces changes throughout the day according to the inhabitants' requirements.

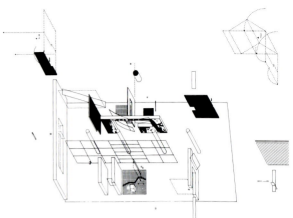

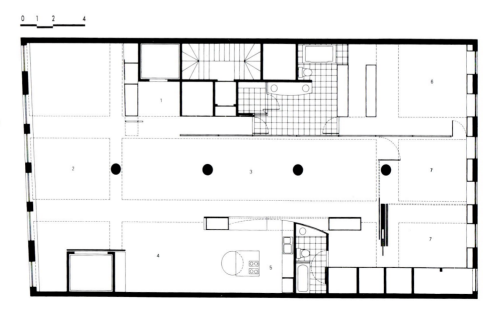

Floor plan
1. Entrance
2. Living room
3. Gallery
4. Dining room
5. Kitchen
6. Master bedroom
7. Guest bedroom

0  1  2  4

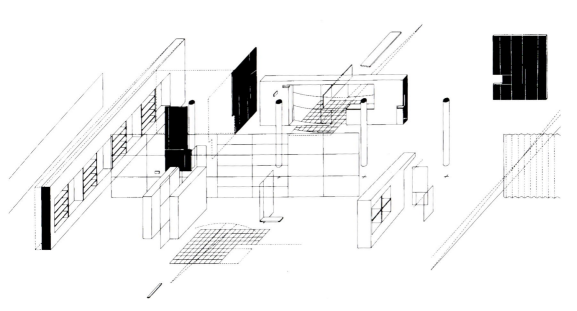

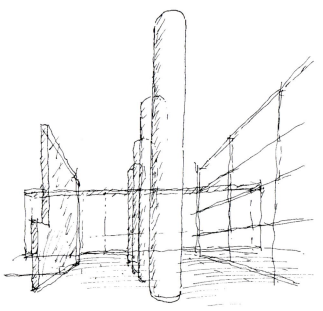

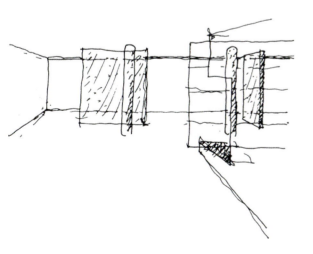

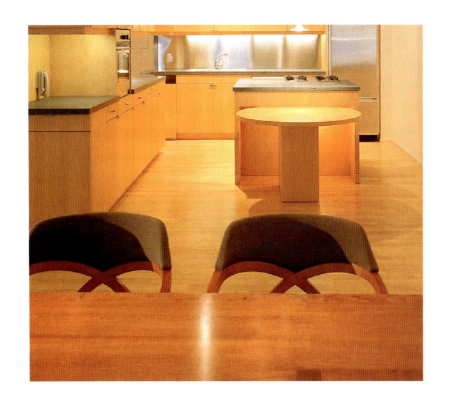

# Christa Prantl & Alexander Runser

Lanzendorfer Mühle

*Mistelbach, Austria*

*Photographs: Margherita Spiluttin*

In this low-budget conversion of a baroque mill located in a small village some 50 km from Vienna, the brief was to establish a large living area on the roof floor of the old storage building, and to create space for a doctor's surgery on the main level. The main level of the residential building was to be remodeled to house the private rooms and a small apartment. The baroque façade was renovated, and the partly-destroyed walls protecting the gardens east and west of the building were re-erected. The facade of the cellar level on the East Side was excavated and found to be an arcade. It is now the entrance to the doctor's surgery. On the west side of the building, a new entrance to the living area was made, providing access to a staircase, which leads up to the new living area in the roof space.

The main intervention is the installation of a new concrete object at the intersection of the storage building and the long residential building. It forms an independent three-dimensional structure with a staircase. Four walls, plates of bare reinforced concrete, define the way into the building. Together with the stairs they are the center of the house. They create a link between the entrance, the private rooms, the new living space on the roof floor, and the surgery in the former storage building. This modern element connects, divides and opens up the older structure, without destroying it.

Two 20$m^2$ glass windows in the roof admit light into the entrance hall, the large living space on the roof floor and the rooms of the surgery. Eight soundproof glass doors separate the surgery from the living space. This, and the soundproof construction of the ceiling, prevent conflict between the doctor's family's living and working spaces. The bare concrete structure helps to separate the living and working areas visually. The physical bulk of this material stores heat, an important factor in maintaining a well-balanced room climate. The space under the glass roof did not require sun protection.

The magnificent assembled wooden structure that supports the sloping roof has been fully restored. The contrast between the varnished wood and the white walls highlights its beauty.

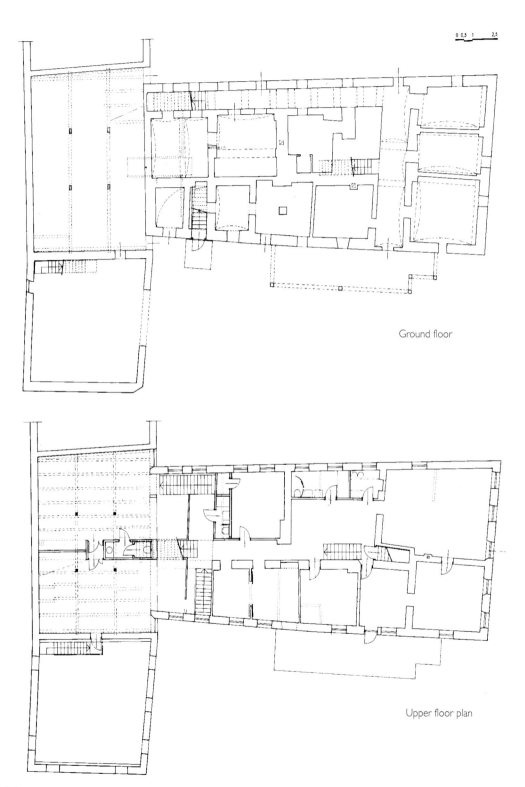

Ground floor

Upper floor plan

The living area situated under the roof receives plenty of natural light through the two large skylights.

West elevation

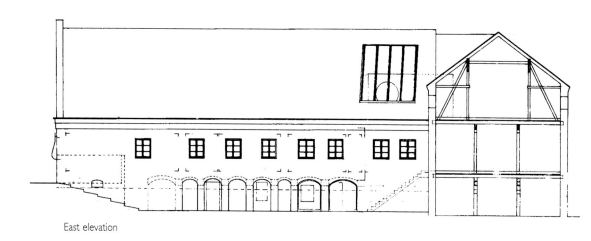

East elevation

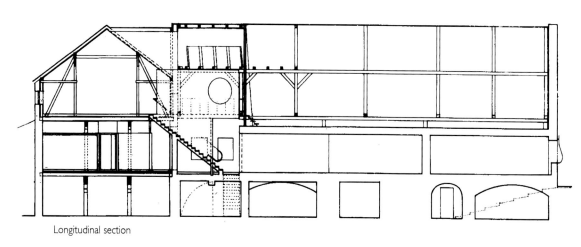

Longitudinal section

# Sergio Calatroni

## Casa Galleria Uchida
### Milano, Italy

*Photographs: Sergio Calatroni*

The project consists in rehabilitating a 90m2 space situated in the city of Milan, in order to adapt it and convert it into a gallery dwelling.

The gallery, in which works of art by the owner of the dwelling are exhibited, is on the first level. This floor are also houses the kitchen and a small bathroom, whereas the whole of the upper floor is taken up by the bedroom and the main bathroom. The lower floor communicates through large French windows with a terrace that provides the space with light.

The whole project is articulated by means of fixed and mobile walls. The kitchen and the bathroom on the lower floor are separated from the gallery by means of a movable panel. The geometric finishes of this panel were made by combining white, black and reddish wood. The floor, a magnificent surface of cherry wood, brings unity to the dwelling. A minimalist staircase of folded sheet leads to the upper floor where the bedroom is located. The two-toned sculptural element that divides the staircase and also performs the function of a banister was made in Greek-work sheet.

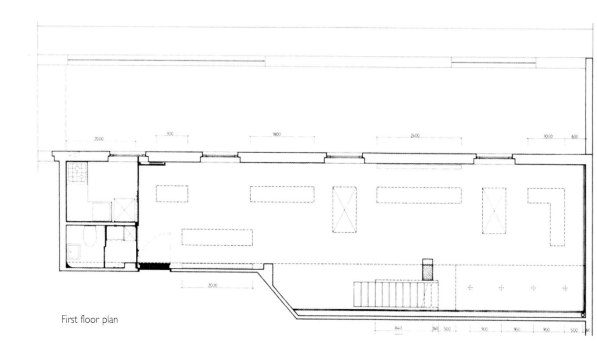

First floor plan

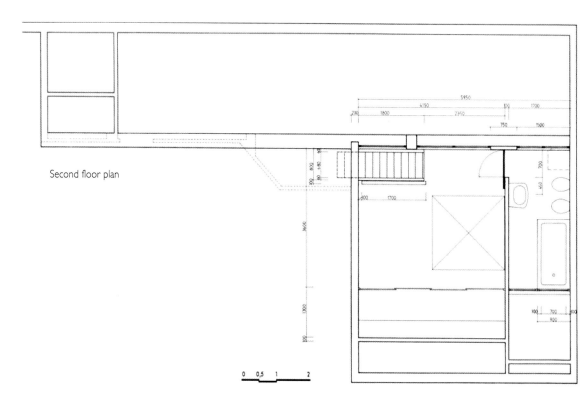

Second floor plan

Cross section

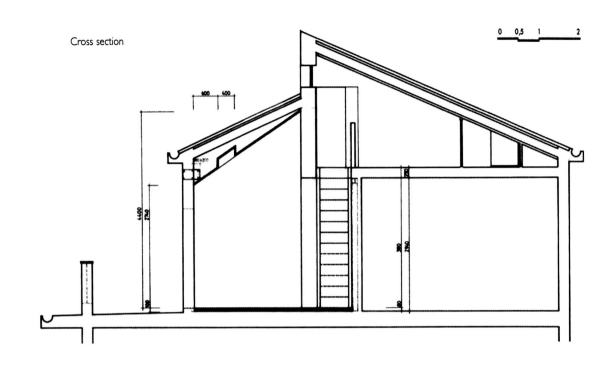

Longitudinal sections of the bathroom

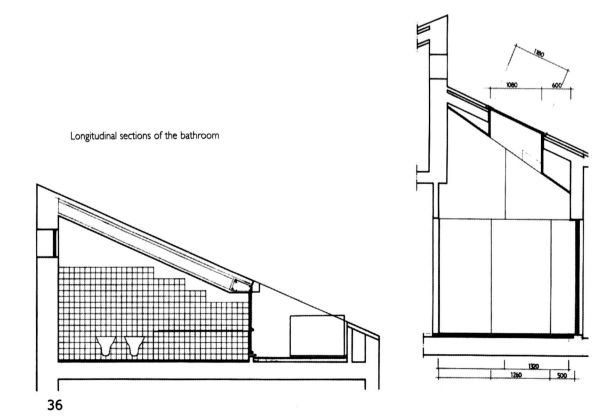

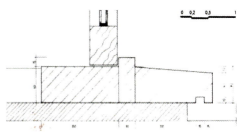

# Circus Architects

## Vaight Apartment
### London, UK

*Photographs: Richard Glover*

The loft has been formed by knocking together two shell spaces to provide one substantial double-height volume, of a scale rarely to be found in central London, where it is located. Carved from the muscular confines of an old printing house the space comes with thick concrete columns and down stand beams and galvanized steel windows of industrial size.

In order to accommodate a family of four, the brief asked for three bedrooms, three bathrooms and as much double space wherever possible.

The solution found by the architects involves the piling up of bedrooms towards the back of the space against the window walls wherever possible.

This spatial organization creates a bright and open space that allows an unconventional way of living. The kitchen area penetrates into the living and dining area, next to closed free-standing volume, which encloses a small study. The upper-level living area overlooks these spaces.

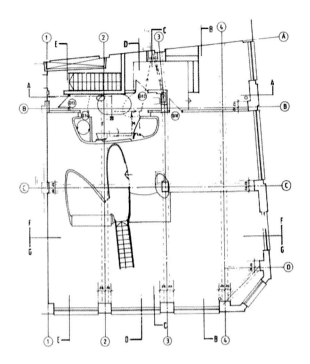

1. Existing fire escape
2. Dressing room
3. Master bedroom
4. Upper reception (on mezzanine)
5. Master bathroom
6. Study
7. Marriet's bedroom
8. Matthew's bedroom
9. Escape corridor
10. Marriet's bathroom
11. Lobby
12. Utility
13. Matthew's bathroom
14. Store
15. Kitchen area
16. Lower reception

Lower floor plan

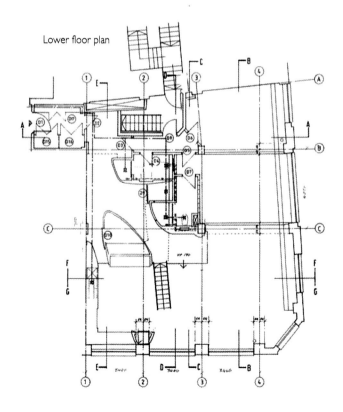

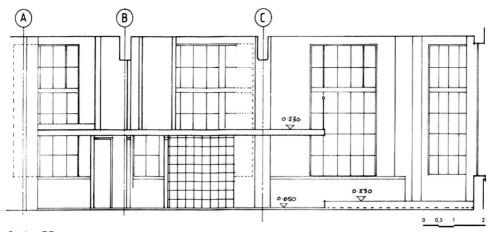

Section CC

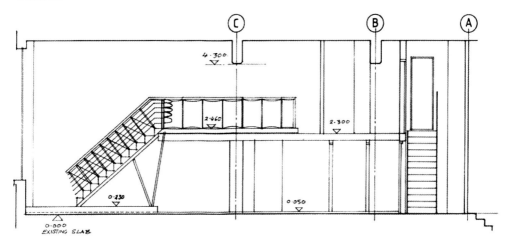

Section DD

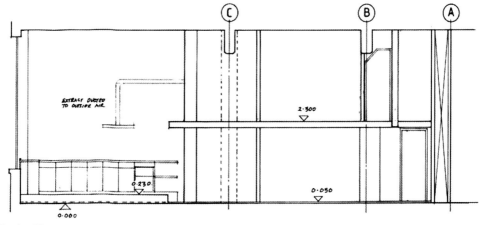

Section EE

# Rüdiger Lainer

*Vienna, Austria*

*Photographs: Margherita Spiluttini*

A two-storey penthouse conceived as a "House on a House": a transparent entity replacing the existing pitched roof, on one of the first reinforced-concrete apartment houses in the city. The site is two minutes from the Stephansdom in the 1st district of Vienna's "holy" area, and has a direct visual link to the cathedral.

The façade of the existing building, built in 1911, imitates the historical character of the street: however, it is in fact despite the fact a concrete building, thereby necessitating a thoroughly modern approach to the penthouse.

Floor plates of exposed profile-metal sheets, as well as a reinforced concrete deck, supported by a steel frame, create a flexible, open space, an allow multiple room configurations. The external skin of stainless steel uprights with clamped glass sheets creates a link between the internal wooden floor and the external planted terraces, with unobstructed views of the dense urban fabric outside.

The project is programed to contain 5 entities, the combination and configurations of which allow the different zones to be used as either living or office space, or a combination of both. Furthermore, laminated glass is used as a roof in the central area to create the conceptual "rift" in the plan, thereby conveniently dividing the intervention into two distinct but interrelated zones. Interior space extends horizontally into the city and vertically to the sky.

Sixth floor plan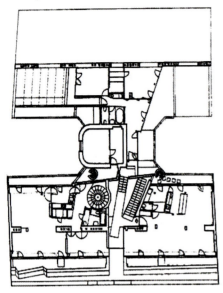

Fifth floor plan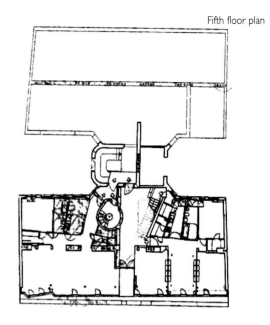

Section 2-2

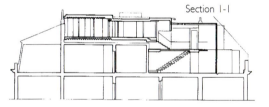

Section 1-1

The open spaces permitted by the use of a light structural system are only interrupted by the service areas.

# Engelen Moore
## House in Redfern
### Sydney, Australia

*Photographs: Ross Honeysett*

This two-storey house has been built on a vacant plot of land formerly occupied by two terrace houses, in a street otherwise composed of houses, warehouses and apartments of varying ages and sizes. The local council insisted that it read as two terrace-type houses rather than as a warehouse. The front elevation is divided into two vertical bays. The major horizontal elements are aligned with the adjoining terraced houses, and each bay relates to these houses proportionally. The internal planning reflects this two-bay arrangement at the front, while the rear elevation expresses the full 6m high, 7m wide internal volume. There was a very limited budget for this project, so a simple strategy was developed to construct a low-cost shell composed of a steel portal framed structure with concrete block external skins on the long sides, lined internally with plasterboard. The front and rear parapets and blade walls are clad with compressed fiber cement sheets. This shell is painted white throughout. Within this white shell are placed a series of more refined and rigorously detailed elements differentiated by their aluminum or grey paint finish. The front elevation is made up of six vertical panels, the lower level being clad in Alucobond aluminum composite sheet, the left hand panel being the 3.3m high front door, and the three panels on the right hand side forming the garage door. The upper level is made up of operable extruded aluminum louvers, enabling it to be adjusted, from transparency to complete opacity.

The 6m high west-facing glass wall is made up of six individual panels, which slide and stack to one side, allowing the entire rear elevation to be opened up. This not only spatially extends the interior into the courtyard, but in combination with the louvered front elevation allows exceptional control of cross ventilation to cool the house in summer, while allowing very good solar penetration to warm the house in winter. In summer, this western glass wall is screened from the sun by a large eucalyptus tree on the adjoining property.

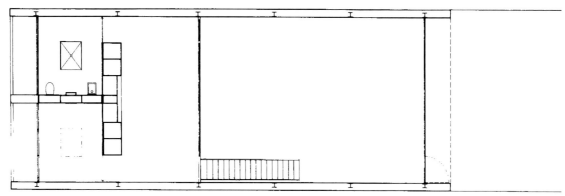

First floor plan

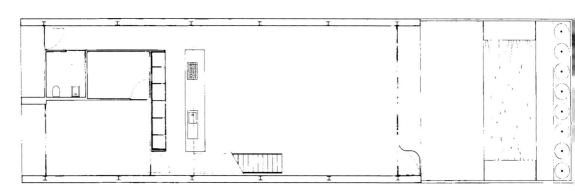

Ground floor plan

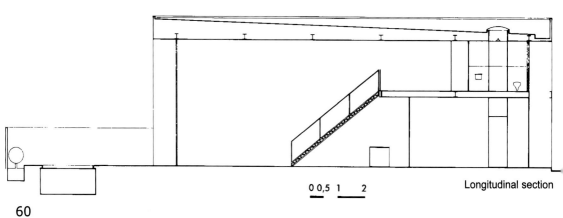

0 0,5 1 2   Longitudinal section

The rooms of the upper floor are fitted with mobile aluminum shutters that can be totally transparent or totally opaque.
The furniture was designed by the architects. The basic premises were low cost and lightness for easy mobility

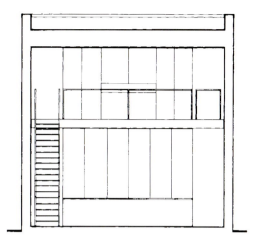

Cross section

# Landau & Kindelbacher

## Housing Conversion

Dachau, Germany

In this project, the architects Landau & Kindelbacher were commissioned to work on two independent flats, situated vertically one on top of the other. The dwellings were joined by cutting an opening in the reinforced concrete floor, thus creating the basis of a roomy duplex apartment. The resulting gap was used to insert a staircase connecting the two levels. Two flights of the staircase are supported by steel plates in the risers, that transmit the loads to a steel structure concealed behind the wooden panelling. The same structure also bears the loads exerted by the stepped beams that support the landings and the third flight of stairs. This arrangement has the additional advantage of providing acoustic insulation from the staircase area's party wall.

The kitchen, which was re-designed, forms a single space with the dining room, although the two can effectively be divided by bringing the sliding glass elements into play. The bathroom areas provided for guests are lined with marble and separated from the adjoining hall by a panel wall with concealed doors. There is also a guest bathroom, which features a lavatory basin and a radiator housed in a marble block.

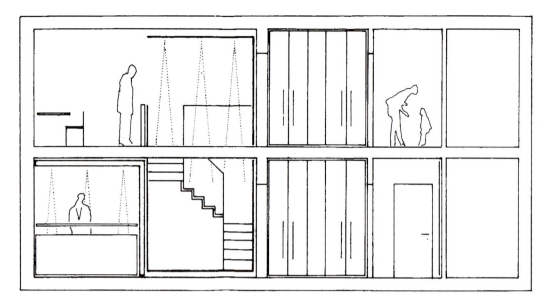

Longitudinal section

Cross section

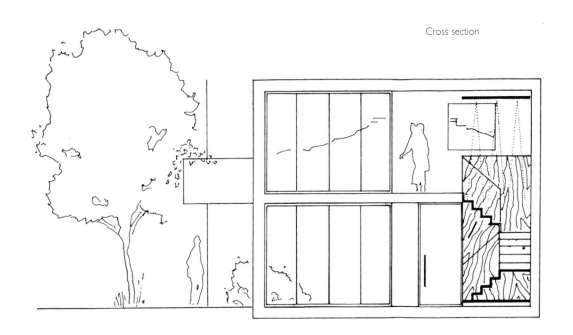

Upper floor plan

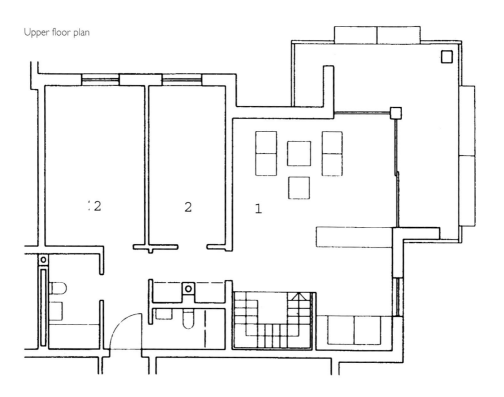

Lower floor plan

1. Living room
2. Room
3. Dining room
4. Kitchen
5. Guest WC
6. Guest bathroom
7. Store with washing machine and dryer

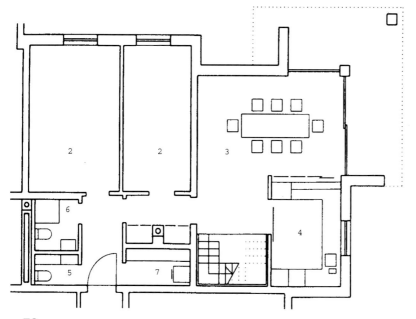

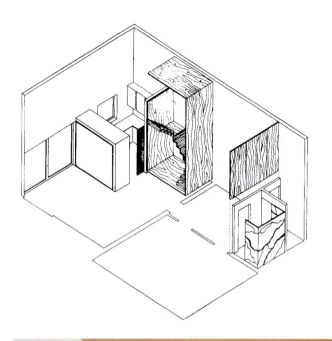

# Cesare Leonardi

Mescoli-Goich House

Modena, Italy

*Photographs: Cesare Leonardi*

The architect decided to erase any past "memory" of interior design so as to be free to explore the potential of a material that had aroused his curiosity – the formwork or shuttering panels used for concrete wall construction. There was also an initial condition: whatever was designed had to come from a single panel, its multiples or sub-multiples, in order to work within a well-defined boundary.

Only one material, one thickness (2.7 cm), one width, one finish, one color (a protective yellow varnish), five standard lengths (100, 150, 200, 300 cm), screws to hold the "solid" together and wheels to move it around were the ground rules. A "solid" originating from the cut and assembly of panel pieces ready for storage and shipping was the goal.

Everything was produced on the same CAD-laser cutter. Once the first few shelves, beds and tables were off the drawing board a previously latent need came to light, that of taking a single panel and, by sectioning it into basic components without wasting anything, to turn it into a chair, and armchair or a stool became ever more insistent.

So the architect started designing solids by tracing their outlines directly onto the panel: the sides flush against one another, the complementary backs and support carved from places that would not weaken the object's utilities. The result was a small armchair whose sides, seat and back-rest consist of pieces so composed as to enable them to develop formally through changes in the original configuration.

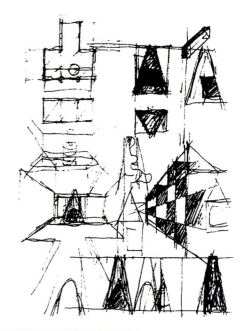

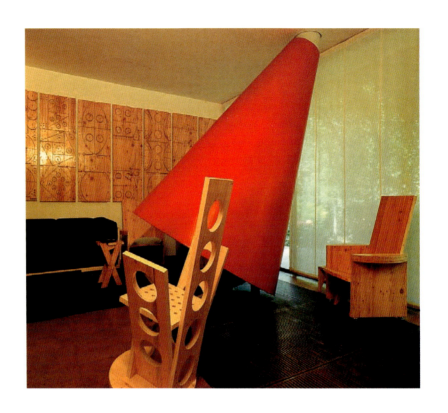

# Adolf H. Kelz & Hubert Soran

## Mittermayer's House
### Salzburg, Austria

*Photographs: Angelo Kaunat*

In the conversion of this two-century-old house near Salzburg the architects have combined two approaches. The original building was divided into two main parts: the original stone building and a wooden shed. The stone building and its internal distribution have been conserved, but the shed has been converted into a big glass box with wooden joinery, within which the rooms hang from the hipped roof.

The glazed box which occupies approximately half of the main building forms the most radical aspect of this scheme. The structural elements of steel and wood are separated from the glazed skin. The living/dining area on the ground floor has an open plan and is overlooked by galleries, while the rooms are white plywood boxes, suspended in the space created within the glass box. All the spaces are independent units integrated into a whole and conjugated by spiral staircases, galleries and walkways that create exciting perspectives. The program includes four bedrooms for the owner's children, a library and a restroom.

The roof has been conserved almost intact, only interrupted by a strip window and a skylight for the loft. It tempers the contrast between old and new and brings unity to the whole. A small refurbished annex with a new zinc roof contains the garage, sauna and some utilities.

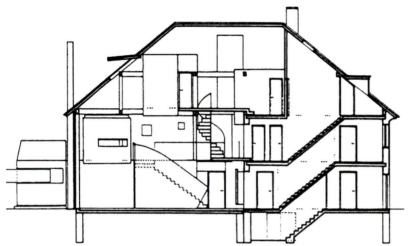

The conventional circulation systems have been replaced by walkways, galleries and spiral staircases that connect the different spaces.

Views of the ground floor living area. The wood and steel structural elements do not touch the façade of the building.

Cross section

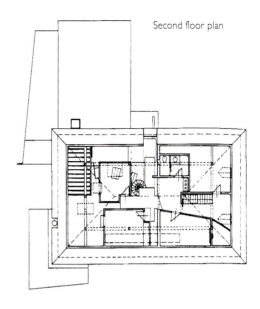

Second floor plan

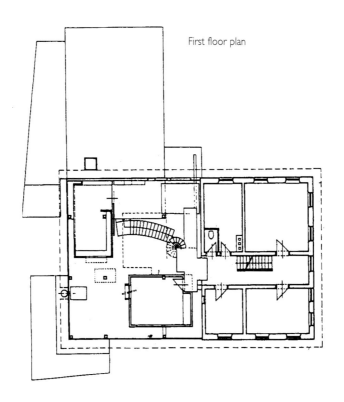

First floor plan

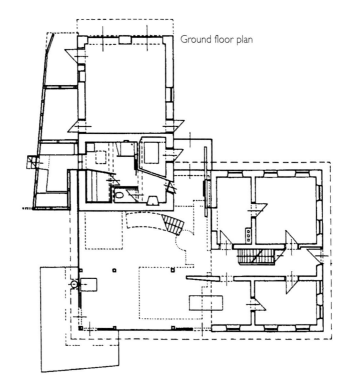

Ground floor plan

# Michael Photiadis

## House in Ekali

Athens, Greece

*Photographs: Imago Tamviskos*

This corner in the suburb of Ekali in Athens belongs to a young couple with frequent house guests. The shape of the site and the wooded opening defined the house's position. The reception areas are centrally located on two levels open to the entrance: bedrooms on the upper floor, and kitchen, service areas and study on the ground floor.

The cylindrical volume fans out to an entrance portico that leads onto the two-storey hallway with a circular skylight. The terracotta color accentuates the outer and inner skin of the cylinder on which the semicircular staircase to the upper floor leans. The circle is completed with a bridge that underlines the boundaries of the hallway and the sitting room of the ground floor, leading east to the master bedroom and west to the guest room.

The two-storey cylinder stabilizes the ninety-degree angle of the house with the abruptly sloping trapezoidal roof of the sitting room and the big opening to the garden. On the east side it connects to the dining space that gives onto the garden. On the west side it flows into the fireplace sitting area with views of the pine trees framing the hearth. The study remains a separate, private space. The kitchen and service rooms function as backstage spaces. The garage below leads to a circular access for mechanical and service spaces near a gym room.

The ground floor reception area is covered with white marble divided by thin black marble joints; the slabs decrease geometrically as the roof lifts up. The hallway's circle is underlined by concentric black stripes on white marble, the dining space has classic black knot paving, while the fireplace sitting area has a parquet floor. The upper floor is covered with a gray wall-to-wall carpet. The sloping ceilings are painted light gray while the roofs are covered with green-black asphalt shingles.

The triangular space of the four-sloped fireplace roof is glazed, while the equal space over the master bedroom wing has a flat roof.

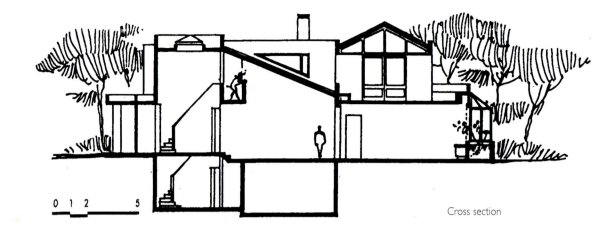

Cross section

# Claudio Silvestrin

Thames Apartment

London, UK

*Photographs: Tessa Robins*

The brief was to redesign the interior of a dwelling belonging to the artists Adam and Carolyn Barker-Mill, a space of 250 m² with one blind wall and three glazed strips. The main factors to be taken into account were the three glazed facades, the presence of thick concrete columns that could not be touched, and the low ceilings.

Leaving the line of the blind wall completely free, Silvestrin arranged the different areas around the three walls giving onto the exterior, thus allowing natural light and views of the city to preside over all the rooms. The landscape and the light seem to flow into the interior, being projected onto the totally white surfaces of the wall and the grey Tuscan stone of the floors. From the entrance hall a gently curving translucent glass screen leads to the living room and conceals the kitchen. Parallel to this route, a more private passage links the bedrooms, kitchen and living room. The two areas are thus functionally separated but have a certain spatial continuity. The translucent screen is repeated in the living room, on the facade facing the river. It acts as a barrier that filters and intensifies the light, creating a dense and evocative atmosphere.

In an exercise of extreme essentiality that is found in all his projects, Silvestrin distributes naked geometrical forms around the dwelling that accentuate the types of material used in each furniture element, from the pearwood benches and tables to the marble piece in which the heating elements are housed, like a clear statement of formal abstraction that results from simplifying function to the maximum, eliminating all secondary elements.

However, a large number of sophisticated details must be resolved in order to achieve a naked space such as this: all the functions and facilities are concealed behind glass screens, inside cupboards and walls. This can be seen in the solid white wall that runs longitudinally through the dwelling, housing the light sculptures of Adam Barker-Mill.

The apartment is arranged around a longitudinal axis that is flanked by a white wall along its whole length. In the foreground, a view of the curved translucent glass screen that separates the hall from the kitchen and directs us towards the living room in the background.

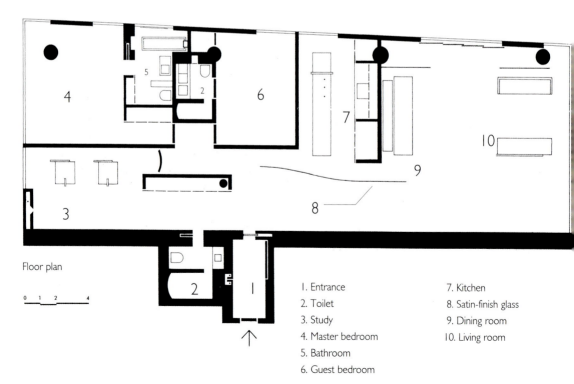

Floor plan

1. Entrance
2. Toilet
3. Study
4. Master bedroom
5. Bathroom
6. Guest bedroom
7. Kitchen
8. Satin-finish glass
9. Dining room
10. Living room

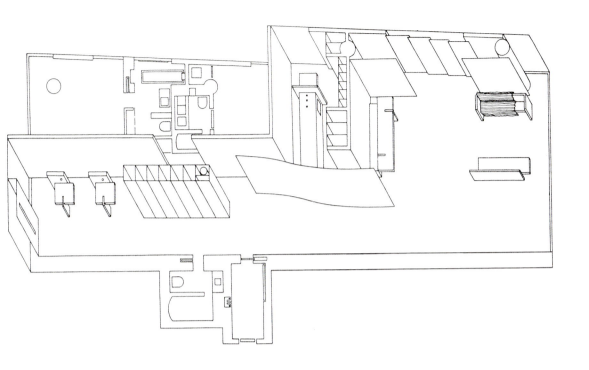

# Marc van Schuylenbergh

## Conversion of Van Schuylenbergh House

Aalst, Belgium

*Photographs: Jan Caudron Anaklasis*

Located in a busy street in the Belgian town of Aalst, the architect Van Schuylenbergh transformed a century-old worker's dwelling into his own home.

In addition to cleaning the facades and opening new windows in the old building, the architect raised a new, long narrow volume that is attached to the old one through an intermediate space in the form of a wedge that follows the curve of the site. This intermediate area is an area of transit in the interior that is well lit from above. The division between the old wing and the new wing is shown by means of a low curving wall.

In the old volume the pure language of the modern intervention is combined with respect for the singularity of some existing elements, such as floor tiles, window frames, fragments of rustic wall face and the old staircase.

The distribution of the rooms has hardly been changed: there are two bedrooms, one situated behind the other, a narrow hall and a staircase.

Another of the most important elements of the new scheme is a raised walkway that communicates the main bedroom with its bathroom, both of which are located on the first floor over each of the two volumes of the dwelling.

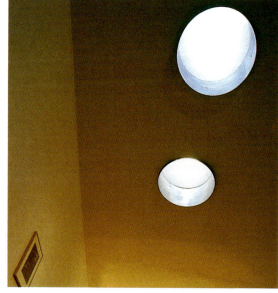

# Arthur Collin architect

## Loft Apartment in Clerkenwell

London, UK

*Photographs: Richard Glover*

The apartment is a single space carefully articulated with a variety of L-shaped forms. The largest 'L' is an uplighting beam that illuminates the whole space and delineates the open areas from the bathroom and foyer.

Beech wood strip flooring with galvanized steel skirting extends through most of the apartment. Wall surfaces are painted plaster or sandblasted original brickwork. The kitchen area consists of two low parallel-galvanized steel cabinets with fine-rubbed black Welsh slate tops. A planter box for herbs sits between the longer cabinet and the adjacent window. Both cabinets sit on a black slate floor. The stainless steel chimney hood over the island cabinet marks the center of this end of the apartment. The absence of other high level cabinets maintains clarity and openness.

At the opposite end of the living area is a square form lit dramatically from below. This monolith contains a wardrobe and conceals the sleeping area, which is raised slightly above the living area.

The glass mosaic-tiled bathroom is the only enclosed space and daylight floods in from the living area through a translucent glazed partition. The full height mirror opposite and the translucent glass counter top further emphasize the lightness and openness. In contrast the dark turquoise tiles of the bath and shower enclosure form a separate intimate alcove. The apartment is deceptively simple in layout but far from minimal. The imperfect nature of the repeated 'L' motif invites colonization by the inhabitants, their personality and their clutter.

The linear east7west alignment of the inserted architectural forms is offset against the three large north facing galvanized steel framed windows. This relationship orients the apartment to the city and the immediate context -the Clerkenwell area of London, which lies between The City of London and the West End.

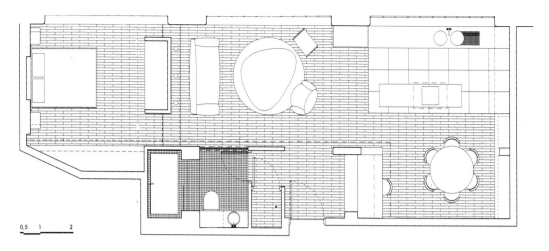

Floor

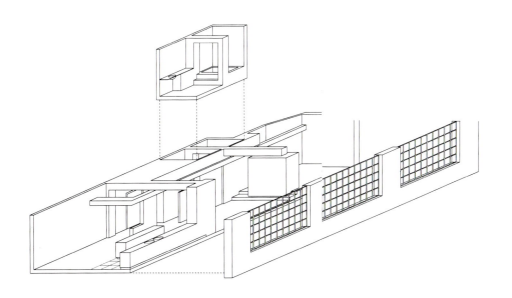

# Valerio Dewalt Train

## Gardner Residence
Chicago, USA

*Photographs: Barbara Karant*

From the very beginning of modern times in America, the traditions of European architecture have undergone an important and symbolic transformation. The substantial elements of traditional design were replaced with architecture of increasing thinness - everything which was substantial became lighter and almost weightless. Thin stud walls of wood and plywood replaced the thick substantial wall of stone and mansory. The Gardner Residence extends this trend to its ultimate conclusion.

The "site" is on the 58th and 59th floor of a Michigan Avenue high rise, and is dominated by the looming dark mass of the John Hancock Tower to the north. The apartment is divided between "ceremonial" and "functional" spaces. In the beginning the apartment was considered as a single space within the enclosing walls. In this space, two idealized boxes were inserted: one of metal, one of wood, one on the first level, the other on the second. These containers define the ceremonial space within the apartment. Each box is impossibly thin, composed of just barely enough substance to retain their form.

In homage to the John Hancock Building, each box is warped by the Tower's imagined gravitational pull. The aluminum shell is defined by a series of straight lines, which are orthogonal either to the city grid or the angled sides of the Tower. The curves of the wood shell are tangential to an imagined circle passing through the four outer corners of the Tower. The leftover space between the walls of these new containers and the outer apartment walls provide the bare minimum of space for the messy, problematic activities of sleeping, cooking, bathing and storage. The details evolved from these basic concepts. Almost every surface of each container is hinged providing access to the different functional areas. The stair to the second floor is so thin it defies explanation. The TV area is both idealized and functional. It has been attached to one of the pivoting metal panels where it functions as part of both the sleeping and bathing area.

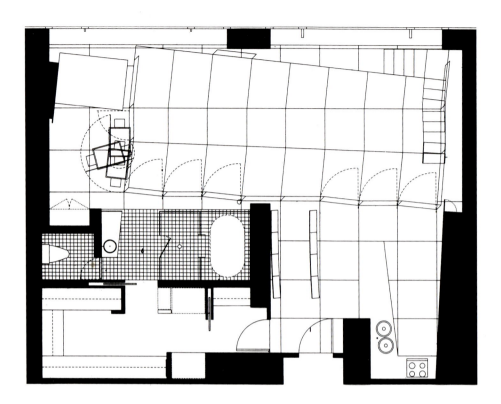

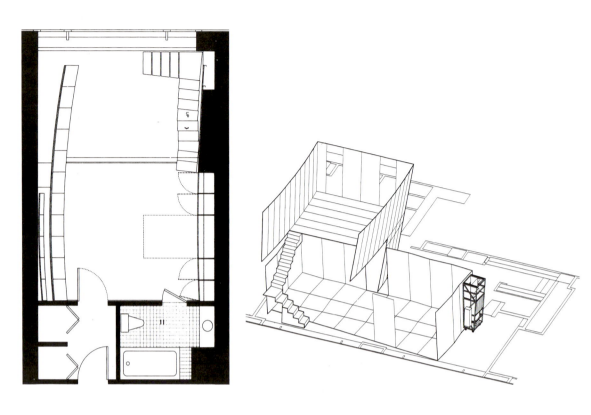

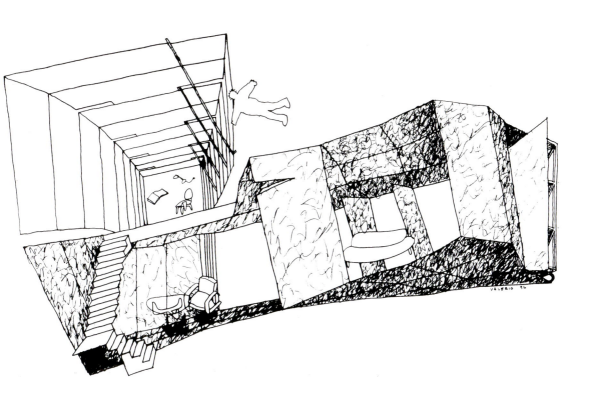

# Rataplan
## Studio flat
Vienna, Austria

*Photographs: Markus Tomaselli*

An entire floor of a former archive in Vienna from the turn of the century was opened up to create a new studio flat. In the original plan only a glass-covered hall illuminated the floor, but a large window now serves as a source of light, creating visual links with the outside world and providing a means of ventilation.

The 4.75-metre-high space is divided by two steel wall slabs that help retain the industrial character of the building and the aesthetics and volume of the hall area. Parallels to these are smaller red panels. This layering effect marks the thresholds to the more intimate zones. The rooms are closed off with full-height sheets of glass, which facilitate visual contacts both internally and externally and maintain the relationship of the rooms with the hall and with the exterior. The space thus gains a new variety of heights and surfaces, new perspectives, lighting, intimacy and openness. The contrast between cool steel and the warm surfaces of the wood floor and the bold red of the wall panels reflects the use of the object as a studio and dwelling.

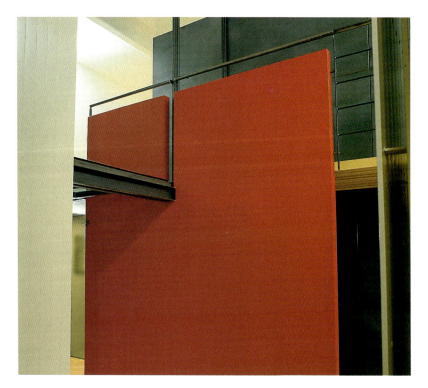

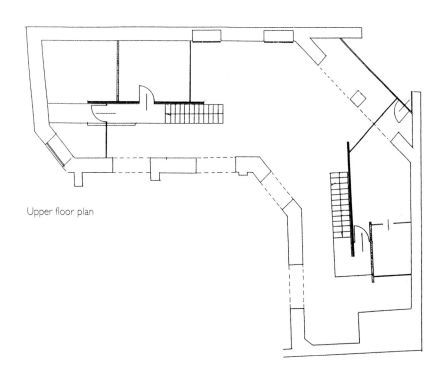

Upper floor plan

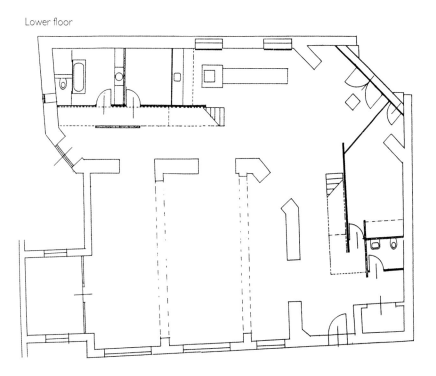

Lower floor

# Simon Conder & Associates

Flat Conversion in Primrose Hill

London, UK

*Photographs: Jo Reid & John Peck*

The client, a barrister and her family, wanted to renovate and enlarge her late 19th century house and patio located in north London. The conversion work was to be undertaken in stages as the resources allowed.

The first stage of the project involved the creation of a private space for the client at the top of house, which would exploit both the unused roof space and the fine views to the rear.

This initial objective was achieved by replacing the original roof with a new steel-framed structure, which incorporated a full-width roof light at the rear. Below this new roof, a steel framed sleeping gallery was inserted with a toughened glass balustrade and a simple staircase in stainless steel and oak.

Below the gallery there is a freestanding translucent oval, containing the bathroom. Its central location provides a degree of separation between the study area at the rear and the living space at the front of the plan. At night, the internally-lit glass oval provides the primary light source for the space as a whole. Materials include painted plaster walls and ceilings, oiled oak floors, sandblasted toughened glass for the walls of the bathroom, teak duck-boarding over an oval fiberglass shower tray for the bathroom floor, and stainless steel for the ironmongery, the support structures in the bathroom and the sanitary fittings.

Gallery plan

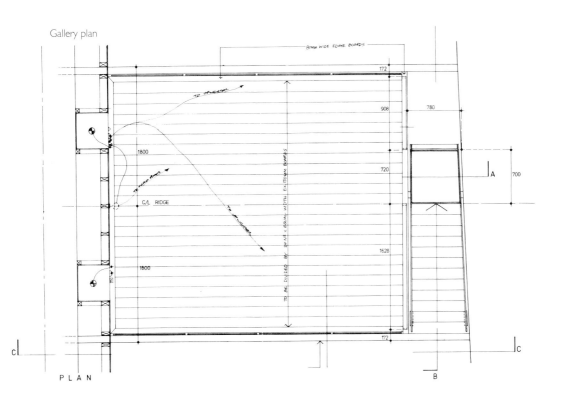

PLAN

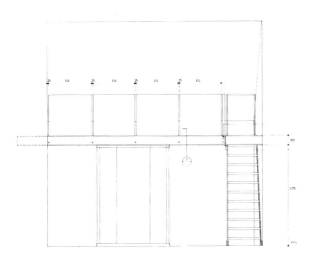

Section CC

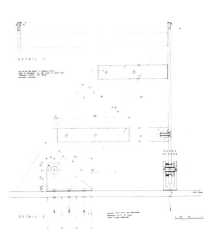

Detail of the stair

# Claeson, Koivisto & Rune

## Apartment in Stockholm
Stockhlom, Sweden

*Photographs: Patrick Engquist*

The task confronting this team of three architects was to create a comfortable, uncluttered living space in a very small area. The apartment, located in the centre of Stockholm, has a total floor area of just 33.5 m², comprised basically of one open-plan room, with adjoining concrete-tiled terrace and blue mosaic-tiled bathroom, connected to the main room by a small opening with a sliding acid-etched window.

Despite its size, the apartment has all the necessary conveniences. Non-living space storage, dishwasher, refrigerator, freezer, microwave and so on are either built-in or concealed behind doors, resulting in a serene and minimalist aesthetic in which to conduct domestic life. Although the work of several designers has been used in the finished project, all the built-in furnishings were designed by the architects themselves.

The terrace furniture can easily be lifted inside for occasions demanding more seating space, and the futon bed doubles up as a sofa. All the lighting and two motorized Venetian blinds are controlled from one centrally placed panel. The Venetian blinds, when shut, hide both the windows and the work desk.

# Torsten Neeland

## House of Dr. Shank
Hamburg, Germany

*Photograph: Klaus Frahm / Contur*

The building, which dates from the beginning of the century, contains an apartment and a doctor's clinic in the centre of Hamburg.

The interior, where both areas are connected, was fully redesigned to optimize the spatial limitations.

An important aim was to keep the furnishing to a minimum in order to allow the space to display its full beauty. Further open space was created by tearing down a separating wall between the library and living room. The architect wished to create a calm environment in which it is easy to concentrate on work and to enjoy the space.

Special attention was paid to the lighting of the apartment, which is of great importance to Neeland and is used as an integral part of the architecture. He believes that it has a magical quality that it can be used to change the atmosphere completely, and that without light architecture is nothing.

The rooms are mostly illuminated indirectly, for example from behind sliding window shades. The flexibility of the shades provides different dimensions of brightness, increasing the perception of space in a limited area.

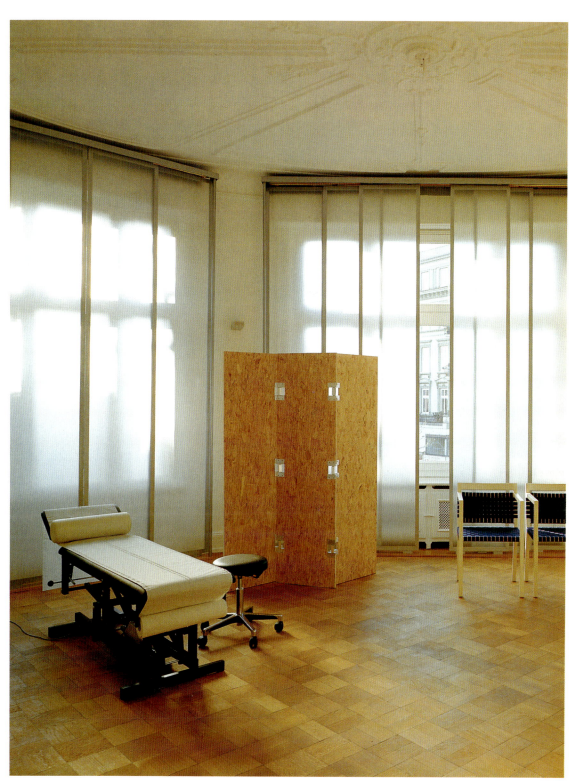

The light penetrates the rooms indirectly thanks to mobile panels that filter it, bathing the rooms in a very intimate atmosphere.

# Fritz & Elizabeth Barth

## Artists' Studios

Stuttgart, Germany

*Photographs: Fritz Barth*

This little row of studios in an east Stuttgart suburb was commissioned by the city to provide 11 artists with an appropriate working and living space. Six two-storey rectangular elements are linked by intermediate semi cylindrical vaults clad in corrugated aluminum; so the whole is like a short irregular necklace with chunky white beads strung together on a silver chain.

The construction is virtually industrial in its simplicity and economy. The rectangular units are of rendered load bearing insulating block work with timber roofs and platforms. Finishes vary, but are usually very economical, with platforms and partitions of industrial grade ply and ground floor finishes of sealed concrete.

The spatial lighting organization of each unit is carefully tailored to the needs of its occupants, but there are some general rules. The rectangular blocks always have double-height top lit spaces as well as galleries and rooms that open into them and are often side-lit. In the vaults, with conservatory-like windows opening to the south, spatial organization is necessarily more limited in scope. But even the vaults show a great deal of variety.

The most eastward unit is almost like a conventional house, with rooms (upper ones linked by bridges over double-height spaces which bring top light into the middle of the plan). Here, uniquely, the bead is linked to the string, and the unit has a chunk of vault as its major workspace. At the other extreme, one of the beads is basically one large volume, with minimal kitchen and bathroom on ground level and a long gallery above.

Section BB'

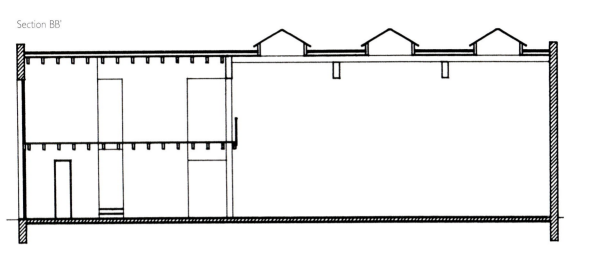

The rectangular blocks house a large double-height space with galleries and rooms that open onto it.

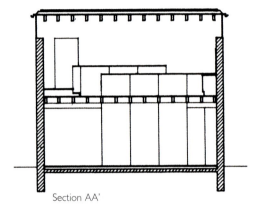

Section AA'

# Giovanni Scheibler

Loft Conversion in Zurich

Zurich, Switzerland

*Photographs: Alex Spichale*

In converting the loft space in this house, the aim was to create extra living space and to bring more light into the top floor flat, while respecting the characteristic turn-of-the-century outward appearance of the building. Ecological and economic factors were also taken into consideration. The architects created a central hall, lit from above by a new roof light set in the ridge of the mansard roof, 7m above the hall floor, There are no fittings that block the path of light: even the gallery floor is of clear glass. Light can also filter through translucent walls into the rooms bordering the hall. Sliding partition elements further help to create space and versatility, in contrast to the usual narrow confines of such flats. The materials used for the new hall are clearly legible against the existing building structure. Anthracite-colored metal, chrome steel and glass stand next to plaster walls and wood. The fine lines of the elements of the hall complement the theme of transparency. The girders supporting the gallery are pairs of tensioned RHS-sections, resting on brackets on the mansard structure.

The cable bracing eliminates any vibrations along the slim sections. The safety glass flooring sheets rest on a double layer of rubber to reduce noise. Chrome steel is used for the handrail and the horizontal cabling. The frame of the sliding partitions is of narrow square tube sections. Between the glazing layers is white glass lining welded to the panes at the side.

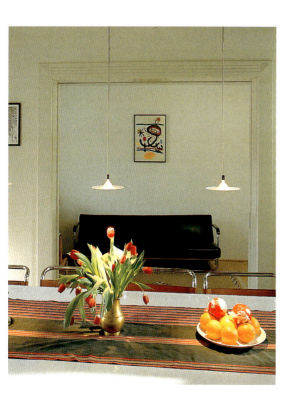

The dwelling is organized around a central hall that is top-lit by a skylight.

The light comes through the translucent glass panels into the rooms surrounding the central hall.

The materials used to build the central hall (steel and glass) are easily recognizable, contrasting with the existing structure of the building.

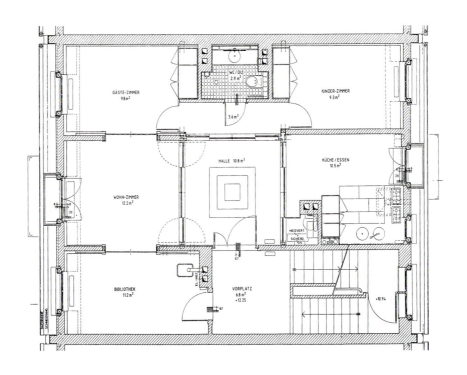

# Paul Robbrecht & Hilde Daem

## The Mys House

Oudenaarde, Belgium

*Photographs: Kristien Daem & Paul Robbrecht*

This house, originally built in the eighteenth-century in a provincial town near Ghent in Belgium has been gradually transformed. It stands on a narrow plot of land on the banks of the river De Scheide at Oudenaarde. To the rear is a lush walled garden and terrace overlooked by a gabled extension and a glass-house. On the street side, a new glass and steel loggia built to replace the gate to the old coach house has been made into the main entrance to the house. It is the external intimation of the changes within; but otherwise, the handsome facade remains intact.

The original building, with later additions, consisted of a sequence of interconnecting rooms stretching back from the street and linked on the ground floor by the glass-house. A cone open to the sky and traversed by a narrow metal bridge penetrates the central part of the house so that light pouring down illuminates the library on the first floor. Open space for the children was created by raising the roof and making a huge attic playroom. On the ground floor, the existing glasshouse was retained and carefully restored, and the kitchen was opened up to the garden by means of a glazed wall and a new window. The coach house is the transition between the street and the light-filled glasshouse. One is made aware of connections in this house, whether the thin bridge drawn through the center of the cone, the sculptural plumbing in the bathroom, or the curving waste-pipes of the kitchen sink; or again, the kitchen stairs leading upwards against the glowing colors of what looks like an old frescoed wall (actually made by sealing fragments of old paint). There has been some restrained use of sumptuous materials. The garden terrace is made of blue Belgian limestone set against concrete tiles. There is a sybarite's bathroom: mirrored on two sides, it is otherwise composed of Carrara marble with a basin of blue Brazilian granite. The house incorporates the works of numerous artists, many of whom, like Lili Dujouri and Juan Muñoz, worked with the architects.

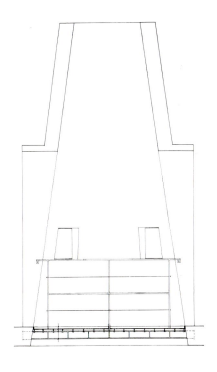

Cross section of the cone of light

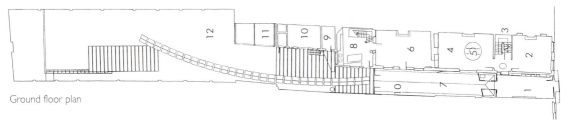

Ground floor plan

1. Entrance
2. Reception room
3. Stairs to the first floor
4. Library
5. Tower
6. Living-room
7. Conservatory
8. Kitchen
9. Boiler room
10. Closet
11. Garden shed
12. Garden
13. Master bedroom
14. Dressing room
15. Master bathroom
16. Access area between rooms
17. Wardrobe-laundry
18. Games room

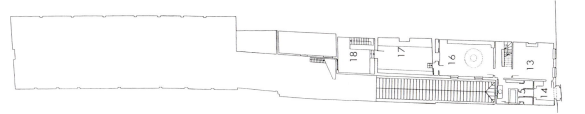

First floor plan

# Ian Hay

Hay Apartment

London, UK

*Photographs: Richard Glover*

Housed in two rooms on the first floor of a modest Georgian terrace off Tottenham Court Road, and occupying only 320ft2, this apartment was designed around the premise that Hay wanted a spacious house in a very small space. He refused to make the compromises usual in studio-sized flats, such as having a shower instead of a bath, or putting the kitchen in the living room. Instead, he began by calculating the minimum space required to cook, or for a double bed, then looked at ways in which these functions could be combined within the limited space.

The flat may have everything, but it is not always where you would expect to find it. The bathroom, for instance, is on a platform above the bed, and from the bath, there is a choice of views: you can open up a hatch to watch a small TV beside the bed, or see through the kitchen into the front room. The front room itself doubles as a work pace, with a large table that folds down from the wall so that Hay can run his practice from home. One key to the success of this very tight conversion is the play on transparency. Neither the bathroom nor the kitchen are treated as enclosed rooms, and surprising sightlines run through the flat, so that the claustrophobic feeling associated with tight, boxed-in spaces is avoided.

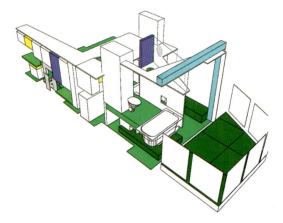

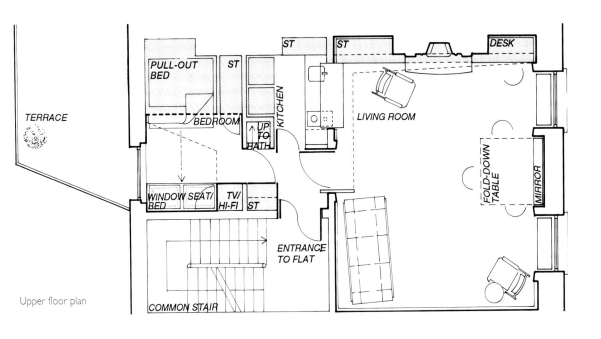

Upper floor plan

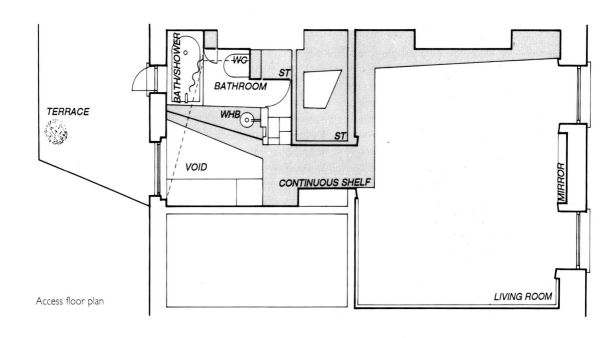

Access floor plan

214

# Hermann & Valentiny

## Anna House

Remerschen, Luxembourg

*Photographs: G. G. Kirchner*

A vintner's house on the Mosel River next door to the Luxembourg office of Hermann & Valentiny was converted for the architect's family. The interconnected rooms and the Lorraine-style architecture were too small scale and narrow to meet the new requirements.

The new design is based on an open spatial conception. Many small spaces became one large flowing space, but old structures and traces of rooms were left legible. A superimposed attic provided additional room for the domestic requirements of the family. Its roof, with the gable in the shape of a pointed arch, lies crosswise to the original ridge. The annexes and superstructures facing the street are of exposed concrete. On the garden side, pergolas and white chalky stucco help new shapes to blend with the old fabric. The new roof is made of wooden beams and covered with galvanized sheet.

Great care was devoted to the preservation and expansion of the garden. Bedded in the orchard and vineyard landscape of the banks of the Mosel, it is an extended living space and the focal point of the studio and the house in good weather.

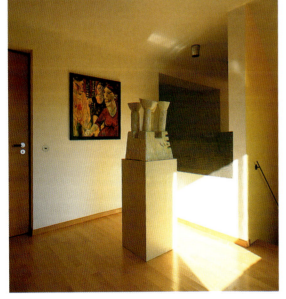

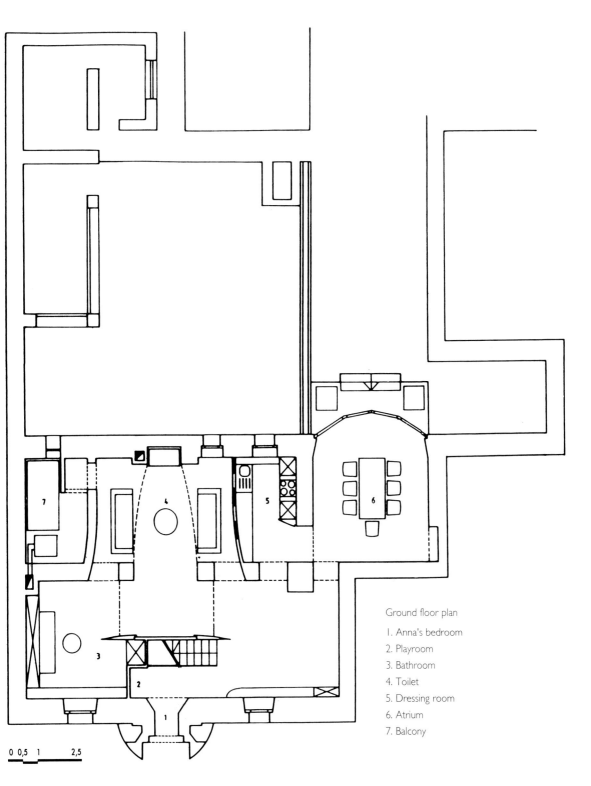

Ground floor plan
1. Anna's bedroom
2. Playroom
3. Bathroom
4. Toilet
5. Dressing room
6. Atrium
7. Balcony

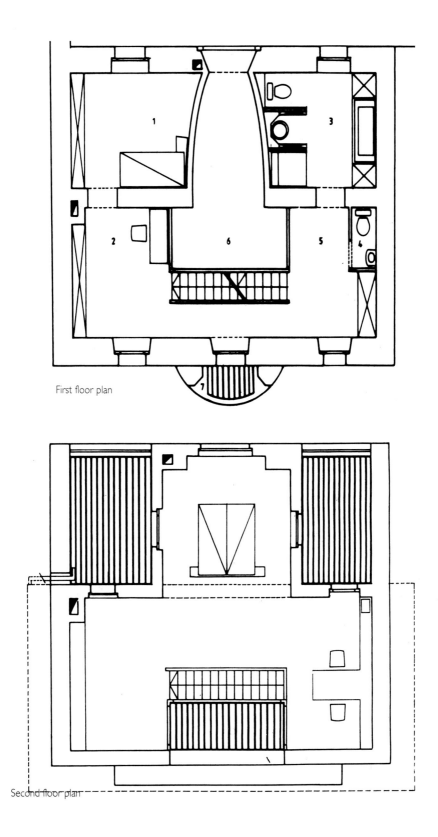

First floor plan

Second floor plan

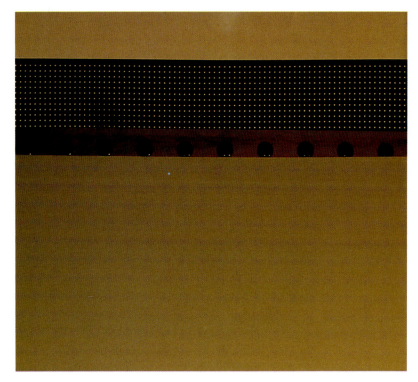

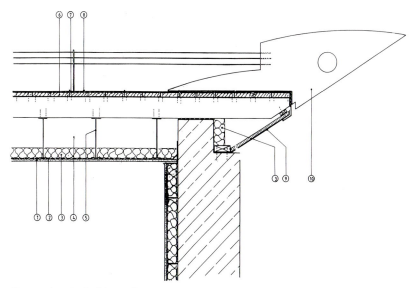

Construction detail of the roof

# Waro Kishi & K. Associates

## House in Shimogamo

Kyoto, Japan

*Photographs: Hiroyuki Hirai*

This two-storey house is located in an urban area at the foot of the Kitayama Mountains in the northern part of Kyoto. Covering almost the entire plot, the house has a frontage 3.2 m × 2 spans and a depth of 4 m × 3 spans. At the core of the steel-frame structure, the architect has created a nakaniwa (inner court) measuring 2 m × 3 spans. The rest of the house consists of a steel frame with exterior walls made of formed cement plates, steel sashes, and large doors. Designing this house, Kishi was fully aware that a contemporary urban house could only convey a sense of reality as a one-off solution to a number of fixed preconditions. At the same time, however, he made an attempt to realize the kind of prototype urban house, that has been a dream of 20th century modernism. He thus focused on incorporating new ideas into planning and structure, which are the most important aspects of modern architecture.

In designing the house, it was not his main intention to secure privacy. Instead the architect placed emphasis on the relationship between the exterior space - that is, the nakaniwa - and the rooms facing it. The result is a large three-dimensional one-room living space, with individual rooms that are independent yet mutually interrelated. Nor did he give preference to the structure. Rather, he considered it as a part of the overall assembly of basic elements, to achieve the impression of a single functional unit. After all, several decades after the mythological age of modern architecture the time may have come to re-think the architecture of the machine age.

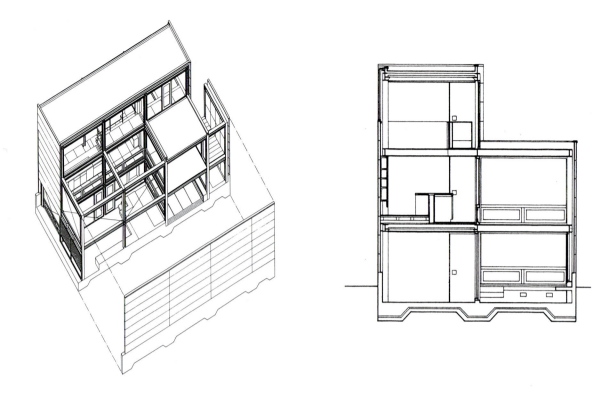

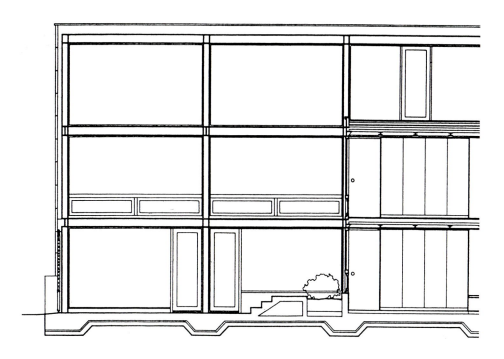

Longitudinal section

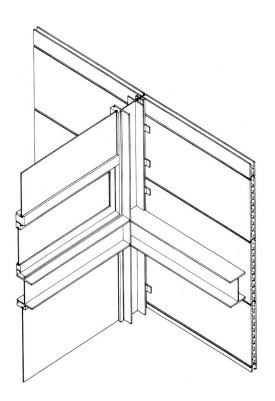

The three-dimensional structure, treated as just another element of the building, gives unity to the functional units of the dwelling.

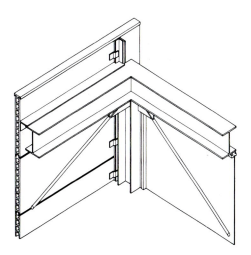

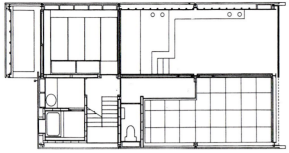

Ground floor plan

Despite the extreme simplicity of the forms and the small number of materials used, the écheme achieves great spatial and volumetric quality.

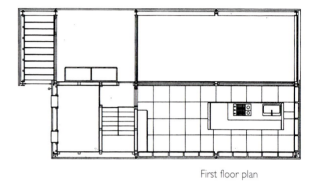

First floor plan

# Eduard Broto

## Studio in Eixample

Barcelona, Spain

*Photographs: Eugeni Pons*

This project by the architect Eduard Broto consisted of rehabilitating an attic located in a 'modernista' (art-nouveau) building in the "right-hand side" of the Barcelona Eixample district. Before the restoration, the attic consisted of a single room used for storage, and a large terrace. The scheme made full use of the possibilities of the premises whilst making a minimum number of changes.

The traditional character of the building has been conserved in the transformation of an obsolete space into a modern functional building.

A wooden element similar to a cupboard was created. It separates and organizes the different zones into which the dwelling is divided. The generous height of the ceiling made it possible to install a half-floor, thus gaining habitable space. The living room is situated at the front of the dwelling, and may be fully opened onto the adjoining terrace. The walls and windows of this main room were decorated with the same 'modernista' floral motif that is found on the stairs of the building.

At the rear of the dwelling are the kitchen, bathroom and a small bedroom. All of the rooms are connected to each other, and are separated only by a sliding door system. The bathroom, the dwelling's principal space, was separated from the rest by means of a decorated glazed partition.

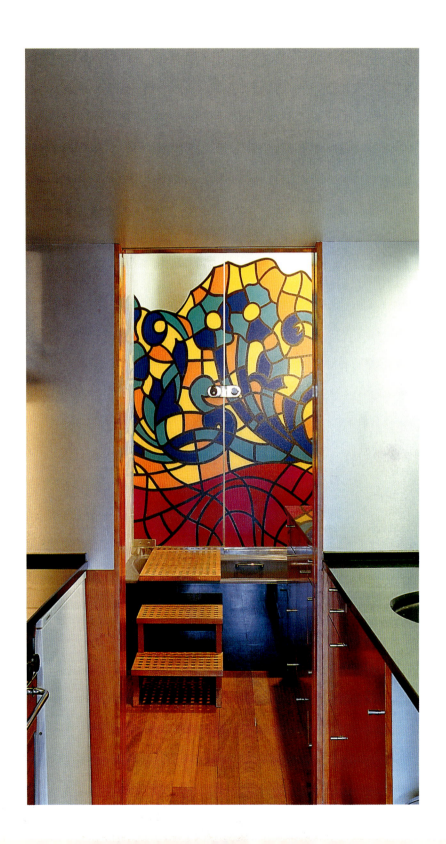

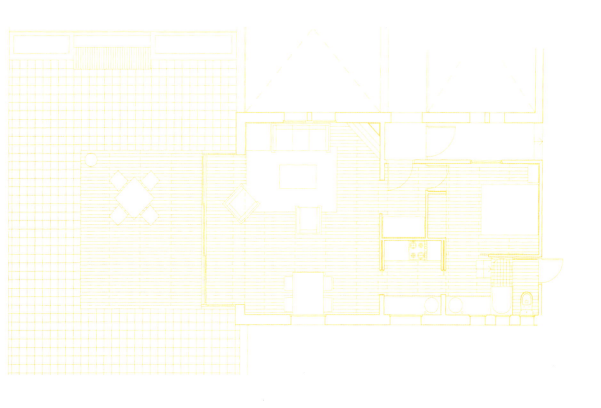

# Massimo e Gabriella Carmassi

Two Apartments in Pisa

Pisa, Italy

*Photographs: Mario Ciampi*

The clients wanted to make two homes for their sons out of a large apartment located on the top floors of a Renaissance building in via S. Maria, which leads from the Arno to the cathedral. Unfortunately, the apartment had been altered at the beginning of this century, and had lost most of its original features. The structures, floor slabs and original spaces were carefully restored, revealing nineteenth-century decorations.

The larger flat is formed by a sequence of rooms overlooking the building's central cloister. To free all the rooms whilst preserving the original structure, a long C-shaped passage was created at a tangent to the cloister, formed in part by an existing corridor. The different insulation requirements of the various spaces were satisfied by differentiating the technological features of door and window frames. Whilst the space adjoining the kitchen is defined by a broken partition of transparent glass with an iron frame, that next to the bedrooms is contains cupboards with large cypress doors and a slightly curved section. The demolition of the entrance corridor floor slab made it possible to create a volume two storeys high. This is overlooked by the large living room and dining room and, on the second level, across a light iron walkway, by the terrace and studio.

The smaller and simpler of the two flats comprises a linear sequence of four rooms. Of varying sizes, these have been conserved and restored according to their original styles, and connected by the old two-leaf wooden doors. A Renaissance-style staircase, built in the 1930s, goes up from the living room to the attic. This consists of three rooms looking onto a very small cloister and a double volume, containing the kitchen and part of the stairs. The complex spatial system comprising the little cloister and the double volume is created through a combination of iron and glass partitions and the bearing wall layout. A skylight illuminates this part of the apartment.

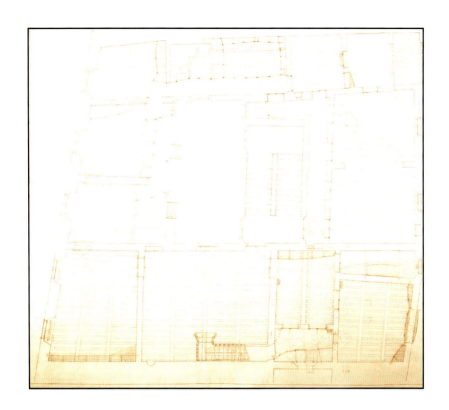

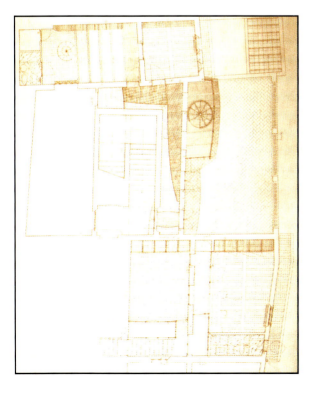

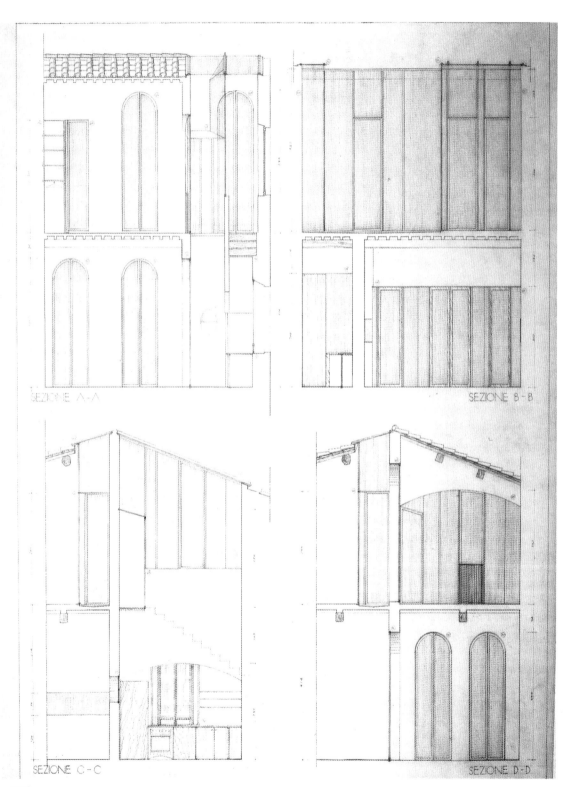

# Apartment A

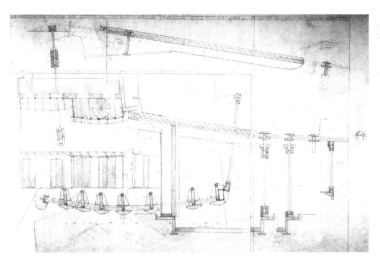

A transparent glass wall separates the kitchen from the corridor. The kitchen cupboards are made of etched glass on a steel structure.

# Apartment B